Women

Body Image and Self-Esteem

A YOUNG WOMAN'S GUIDE
TO CONTEMPORARY ISSUES™

Women
BODY IMAGE AND SELF-ESTEEM

MARY-LANE KAMBERG

ROSEN
PUBLISHING®

New York

For Audrey Phillips

Published in 2013 by The Rosen Publishing Group, Inc.
29 East 21st Street, New York, NY 10010

Copyright © 2013 by The Rosen Publishing Group, Inc.

First Edition

Library of Congress Cataloging-in-Publication Data

Kamberg, Mary-Lane, 1948–
 Women: body image and self-esteem/Mary-Lane Kamberg. — 1st ed.
  p. cm. — (A young woman's guide to contemporary issues)
Includes bibliographical references and index.
ISBN 978-1-4488-8399-8 (library binding)
1. Women — Health and hygiene. 2. Beauty, Personal. 3. Self-esteem in women. 4. Self-perception in women. I. Title.
RA778.K34 2013
613'.04244 — dc23

2012018937

Manufactured in the United States of America

CPSIA Compliance Information: Batch #W13YA: For further information, contact Rosen Publishing, New York, New York, at 1-800-237-9932.

Contents

INTRODUCTION

You are smart. Pretty. And important. Just the way you are.

If a small voice inside you just whispered, "No, I'm not," this book is for you.

You are not alone.

One study reported by the National Institute on Media and the Family found that 78 percent of seventeen-year-old girls are "unhappy with their bodies." The negative body image doesn't begin then. In a National Heart, Lung, and Blood Institute study, 40 percent of girls between the ages of nine and ten have tried to lose weight. According to a study by the University of Minnesota, as many as 88 percent of teen girls have a negative body image, and 85 percent say they "worry a lot about their appearance."

It's no wonder. Print, broadcast, film, and digital media bombard them with unrealistic images of "ideal" bodies that have little resemblance to teen girls in real life. Media presents a goal that is impossible to achieve. The awkward stage called puberty presents additional dilemmas as the body changes at its own pace and in ways that may differ from those of peers.

In pursuit of perfection, girls sometimes suffer severe damage to their body image and self-esteem. Many girls come to believe that they don't matter—that they'll never be "good enough." This inaccurate belief affects their relationships with peers, romantic interests, and adults. They may fall victim to others who take advantage of them or use them as sex objects.

Poor body image and low self-esteem also affect the ways they communicate with others. They hang back in social situations. They refuse to voice their opinions. Worse, they become unable to voice their own wants and needs.

In some cases, they resort to self-inflicted harm from such eating disorders and self-injury as anorexia, bulimia, cutting, burning, and other behaviors designed to punish themselves or inflict physical pain. They may risk their own health—and even lives. They are their own worst enemy.

However, girls can build self-esteem and repair negative body image either by themselves or with professional help. By focusing on good nutrition and an active lifestyle, they can survive these teenage woes and turn their sights on future happiness and success.

ABUSE Success EATING DISORDER dieting SEXUALIZATI
NUTRITION body image WOMEN SELF-ESTEEM Exerci

One way is to participate in school activities and the social life around them. Another is to look for positive role models. By reaching outside themselves, they can achieve a sense of belonging and take their rightful place among their peers.

If you are experiencing any of these stresses, learn all you can. Find out how to help yourself. Seek help from parents, teachers, or professionals. And take steps to free yourself from behaviors—and even addictions—that keep you from reaching your potential greatness.

If you know someone else who falls into this category, take action. Be a supportive friend. If necessary, tell a trusted adult and ask for help.

ABUSE EATING DISORDER
Success WOMEN
SEXUALIZATION
SELF-ESTEEM body image
dieting
NUTRITION Exercise

CHAPTER 1

MEDIA BOMBARDMENT

No sooner had the movie *The Hunger Games* opened to blockbuster crowds than film critics commented on actress Jennifer Lawrence's weight. The slender Academy Award nominee (for best actress in *Winter's Bone*) plays the female lead, Katniss Everdeen. The character comes from a poor district where people are starving.

The critics said she was "insufficiently malnourished," had "lingering baby fat," and was a "fairly tall, big-boned lady." The worst: she was "too big" for her romantic interest, played by Josh Hutcherson. Yet, no one mentioned the physique of Liam Hemsworth, whose character hailed from the same district. Hemsworth stands well over six feet (182 centimeters) and weighs around 190 pounds (82 kilograms).

Lawrence is not the only celebrity condemned by critics. Singer Miley Cyrus has also been attacked for being "fat." She defended herself on Twitter. She posted a photo of a woman with an obvious eating disorder and tweeted, "By calling girls like me fat, this is what you're doing to other

FILM CRITICS CONDEMNED JENNIFER LAWRENCE FOR BEING TOO FAT FOR HER ROLE IN *THE HUNGER GAMES*. NO ONE MENTIONED THE PHYSIQUES OF COSTARS JOSH HUTCHERSON (*ABOVE*) OR LIAM HEMSWORTH.

USE Success EATING DISORDER dieting SEXUALIZATION
NUTRITION body image WOMEN SELF-ESTEEM Exercise

people." She also posted a picture of Marilyn Monroe with the tweet, "Proof that you can be adored by thousands of men even when your thighs touch."

Body image is the way you feel about your own physical appearance. A negative body image may include self-criticism of your body, weight, or specific body parts. You might even dislike such things as your hair, skin color, or facial features. The media is largely to blame. Movies, television, music videos, magazines, and advertising bombard girls with messages that "pudgy isn't pretty" and "boys only like thin girls." It's no wonder teenage girls (and those even younger) have trouble with body image.

WHAT ARE YOU WATCHING?

Recently, television show *Entertainment Tonight* featured a segment on a new Lifetime reality show, *Starving Secrets with Tracy Gold*. The featured show follows girls with eating disorders as they progress at treatment centers.

The *Entertainment Tonight* segment featured real girls binging and purging. It also showed near-death photos of anorexic model Isabelle Carol. The commercials that aired

AT 5 FEET, 8 INCHES (173 CM) TALL AND 125 POUNDS (57 KG), CANADIAN MODEL AND ACTRESS SHAY MITCHELL PORTRAYS AN "IDEAL" IMAGE OF BEAUTY THAT FEW TEENS IN REAL LIFE CAN ACHIEVE.

during the show included one from Hy-Vee, where handsome Australian chef Curtis Stone cooked a big Thanksgiving meal. During the commercial, the author and TV personality frequently told viewers to keep the food low fat and calorie friendly. Another commercial promoted Lee Slender Secret jeans that make women look "ten pounds slimmer."

Typical Hollywood heroines and Disney princesses have small waists, long legs, and large busts. Video games, comic books, and cartoons also promote female superheroes with unrealistic body types. And what about Barbie dolls?

Teen magazines keep the bombardment coming. According to the National Institute on Media and the Family, every third article in magazines aimed at teenage girls focuses on appearance. Topics include how to dress, apply makeup, and exercise to remove body flaws. And half of the ads in those magazines appeal to the desire for beauty. They often feature underweight females with muscular males. Photos are touched up, removing wrinkles, fat, and pores so the

models look "perfect." They are sending a false message: beauty brings love, wealth, and happiness. It doesn't.

NOT GOOD ENOUGH?

Girls may compare their own bodies with the ones they see in the media. Many come to the conclusion that they don't measure up. They don't realize what models and celebrities do to look perfect. Media darlings need

MAGAZINES FOR TEENAGE GIRLS EMPHASIZE APPEARANCE WITH ARTICLES ABOUT MAKEUP, FASHIONS, AND EXERCISES TO ELIMINATE BODY FLAWS. HALF OF THE ADS APPEAL TO A DESIRE FOR BEAUTY.

help from personal trainers, stylists, makeup artists, plastic surgeons, and friendly photographers who touch up their photos. In reality, stars don't really look like their media images.

Girls with a negative body image can become preoccupied with weight and dieting—and can even develop eating disorders. They may avoid physical activities, thereby reducing their general fitness. They may lose interest in school. Or, they may harm themselves with alcohol or other drugs or participate in unsafe practices or sexual activity. Their negative body image often leads to low self-esteem.

SELF-ESTEEM

Self-esteem is the way you value yourself. Healthy self-esteem means you accept yourself the way you are. It helps you make friends, develop independence, and challenge yourself—both physically and mentally. On the other hand, low self-esteem has negative effects. Girls as young as elementary school age already see the body as a measure of self-worth.

Girls with low self-esteem lack social skills and avoid social activities. Some suffer from anxiety, depression, or eating disorders. They are generally pessimistic. They fail to recognize their own potential. They minimize their accomplishments. They greet compliments with negativity. Some are afraid to assume responsibilities or form their own opinions.

People with low self-esteem never feel "good enough."

They often:

- Think negative thoughts about themselves
- Avoid trying new things
- Compare themselves to others in a negative way
- Have a hard time making friends or participating in social activities
- Feel sad or depressed
- Discount compliments as unwarranted
- Feel jealous
- Put themselves down
- Dwell on past mistakes

 # THE HEALTHY MEDIA FOR YOUTH ACT

In 2010, the Girl Scouts of the USA developed a bill known as the Healthy Media for Youth Act (H.R.2513/S.1354). The proposed law encourages girls and women to reject negative media images. It establishes a national task force to develop voluntary media guidelines to promote positive images of girls and women. It supports age-appropriate education about the negative effects of the sexualization of women and promotes research about the effects of media images on young people.

The bill died in committee during the 111th Congress (2009–2010). However, U.S. representative Tammy Baldwin (D-Wisconsin) and U.S. senator Kay Hagen (D-North Carolina) reintroduced it during the 112th Congress (2011–2012). Academy Award–winning actress Geena Davis lent her voice in support. The bill is still pending.

USE Success EATING DISORDER dieting SEXUALIZATION
JTRITION body image WOMEN SELF-ESTEEM Exercise

THE EFFECTS OF PUBERTY

Puberty doesn't help. It's a decidedly awkward stage where everyone—yes even the most popular girl in school—feels unattractive at times. To make things worse, puberty is a time when girls are most likely to compare themselves with others.

Many girls gain weight as their bodies change shape. Each person's genetic makeup affects this stage of development. Some girls develop early compared to their peers. Others develop later. Either way, girls may feel uncomfortable or embarrassed about what their bodies are doing—or not doing. As the body changes, the perceived failure to measure up may become magnified. During puberty—and later—girls have trouble accepting the idea that healthy body shapes vary. Also, puberty is a time of extreme emotions. Low self-esteem at this phase can lead to depression, violence, pregnancy, delinquency, mental or physical disorders, or suicide.

All of this occurs at a time when girls have a strong desire to fit in with peers. Media messages tell them that the way to be accepted is to meet impossible-to-achieve beauty standards and to be "hot."

EFFECTS OF SEXUALIZATION

Overall, the media portrays females as sex objects who wear revealing clothes and pose with enticing body posture and facial expressions. Do these visuals offer skewed messages about beauty, health, nutrition, and reality? Many experts think so.

A task force report from the American Psychological Association says sexualization and objectification undermine self-confidence. Sexualization is an emphasis on sexual appeal or behavior in determining self-worth. It places no value at all on other characteristics. Objectification is thinking of or presenting something as an object. In other words, it turns a girl into an object for another's sexual use.

One major effect of unrealistic media images is the sexualization of girls and young women. Sexualization and objectification have negative effects on important aspects of life. They can lead to such emotional problems as shame and anxiety. The report also links sexualization with depression, eating disorders, and low self-esteem. And it suggests that sexualization interferes with development of a healthy sexual self-image.

"REAL WOMEN"

Unrealistic images exaggerate the viewer's focus on physical appearance over character, intelligence, humor, compassion, or accomplishment. In real life, women come in a wide variety of shapes and sizes—just like their individual personalities. In fact, only 5 percent of American women have the same "ideal" body type featured in advertising, according to the National Association of Anorexia Nervosa and Associated Disorders. Even plus-size models often are thinner than the average woman.

Some companies and organizations are working to reverse this trend. In 2004 Dove, a skin cleanser brand from Unilever, conducted a major worldwide study, *The*

FOR DOVE'S CAMPAIGN FOR REAL BEAUTY, LAUNCHED IN 2004, ART DIRECTORS USED PHOTOS OF "REAL" WOMEN OF DIFFERENT SHAPES AND SIZES, FLAWS AND ALL.

Real Truth About Beauty: A Global Report. The company revisited the topic with follow-up research in 2010.

Results of the most recent study show that out of more than 1,200 girls ages ten to seventeen, 72 percent feel tremendous pressure to be beautiful. In a narrower group

ABUSE Success EATING DISORDER dieting SEXUALIZAT
NUTRITION body image WOMEN SELF-ESTEEM Exerc

of girls ages fifteen to seventeen, more than 70 percent of those with a negative body image said they avoid normal daily activities. They stay home from school, refuse to go to doctor appointments, or even refrain from sharing their opinions.

The 2010 study also found that while 80 percent of women around the world say that every woman has something about her that is beautiful, they don't see their own beauty. Other results included:

- Only 4 percent of women consider themselves beautiful.
- Only 11 percent of girls would use the word "beautiful" to describe themselves.

According to Dove's Web site, "research shows that it is still important for us to address girls' anxiety about looks,

USE Success EATING DISORDER dieting SEXUALIZATION
UTRITION body image WOMEN SELF-ESTEEM Exercise

as there is a universal increase in beauty pressure and a decrease in girls' confidence as they grow."

The 2004 study prompted the brand to launch the Campaign for Real Beauty. It used real women without the stereotypical traits that seemed to define beauty in other media. The next year, the campaign featured six women with "real curves" to counter prevailing wisdom that only thin is beautiful. In 2006 Dove created the Self-Esteem Fund. It was used to teach and inspire girls and women to accept a wider definition of beauty. Since then Dove has created educational programs and activities that help girls build self-esteem. By 2010 the company said these programs had reached more than seven million girls. The goal is to reach fifteen million girls by 2015.

A different project, the Confidence Coalition promotes self-confidence in girls and women. It's an international movement started in 2009 by the Kappa Delta Sorority. The group encourages girls and women to "stand up for healthy, balanced, and positive images of girls and women in media." The sorority also created International Girls Day, which is celebrated each year on November 14. Activities for the day encourage girls to build self-confidence. The group hopes the celebration will inspire girls to realize their dreams.

New Media Images

Although such celebrities as the Hiltons, the Kardashians, and the women from *Jersey Shore* seem to send a message that includes a twisted sense of reality, beauty, and value, other celebrities have succeeded in breaking

America Ferrara's role as the lead in ABC's *Ugly Betty* helped break through the Hollywood stereotype of glamorous women. Other pioneers include Christina Hendricks, Queen Latifah, and Sara Ramirez.

USE Success EATING DISORDER dieting SEXUALIZATION
JTRITION body image WOMEN SELF-ESTEEM Exercise

through Hollywood stereotypes. One is Christina Hendricks, best known for her role as Joan Holloway on *Mad Men*, a series on the AMC cable channel. She is a curvy woman who has been called "a new modern ideal of Hollywood glamour" and a role model for full-figured women. She's been compared to such former stars as Marilyn Monroe, Jane Russell, and Veronica Lake. In 2010 female readers of *Esquire* magazine named her the "sexiest woman in the world."

America Ferrara is another actress who is helping to change media stereotypes. Early in her career she starred in the film *Real Women Have Curves*. Later, in the lead

PLASTIC SURGERY AND TEENS

Your ears stick out. Your nose is too big. Your boobs are too small—or too large. Should you consider plastic surgery?

According to the Confidence Coalition, 90 percent of all women want to change something about their physical appearance. Many want to look younger or sexier. However, among teens the reason often is simply to "fit in." For some, plastic surgery can restore self-esteem, self-confidence, and self-empowerment. Depending on the teen's reasons, expectations, and maturity, surgery may be appropriate.

According to the American Society of Plastic Surgeons, nearly 219,000 patients between the ages of thirteen and nineteen had plastic surgery procedures in 2010. Ear surgery was the most popular. Other types included nose reshaping, correction of breast asymmetry, and breast reduction or augmentation.

ABUSE Success EATING DISORDER dieting SEXUALIZA NUTRITION body image WOMEN SELF-ESTEEM Exerc

role in the ABC TV series *Ugly Betty*, she played a girl with braces, bushy eyebrows, and messy hair instead of a glamorous character. Her work was so well-received that she has won Emmy, Golden Globe, and Screen Actors Guild awards for comedy.

Queen Latifah, an award-winning singer and actress, is another buxom woman whose size has not hindered her success. She has won a Golden Globe award, two Screen Actors Guild Awards, two Image Awards, and a Grammy Award. She has also been nominated for six more Grammys and an Academy Award. She has served as a spokesperson for Cover Girl cosmetics, Curvation ladies underwear, Pizza Hut, and the Jenny Craig weight management company.

Sara Ramirez, who plays orthopedic surgeon Callie Torres on *Grey's Anatomy*, describes herself as "a size twelve in a size zero world." She has also been labeled a "Latina" actress, which carries its own set of stereotypes, notably that they are "curvy." She has said that she has played a part in that. However, she knows that there also is a positive side, too.

She told HuffPost Celebrity, "I do understand how there is a teenager somewhere in America who is feeling bad about herself because she has curves. Then she sees a woman who has curves playing a doctor—an intelligent doctor on TV who is flawed and lovable and going through her life just like everybody else—and she identifies with her and feels better about herself. There is the positive side to it too."

ABUSE   EATING DISORDER

Success   WOMEN

SEXUALIZATION

SELF-ESTEEM   body image

dieting

NUTRITION   Exercise

CHAPTER 2

COMMUNICATION AND RELATIONSHIPS

Have you been teased or heard negative comments about your looks? Such behavior is never "well-meaning" or "just a joke." It can affect the way you feel about your body and yourself.

The messages you receive from others—and the ones you send yourself—affect your body image and self-esteem. Have you ever told yourself the same hurtful things you're afraid someone else will say?

- I'm having a bad hair day.
- My belly sticks out over my jeans waistband.
- I'm too stupid to balance a checkbook.
- My thighs are too fat to go to the pool.

Often women are their own worst enemies. In fact, Dove's worldwide research found that 54 percent of women say they are their own worst beauty critic. If you're

TECHNOLOGY OFFERS NEW TOOLS FOR BULLIES, WHO MAY USE MOBILE PHONES OR SOCIAL MEDIA WEB SITES TO SEND EMBARRASSING OR HARMFUL MESSAGES TO THEIR VICTIMS.

struggling with your own self-esteem, why contribute to the issue with negative self-talk?

Beyond that, strong social ties are important. Everyone needs the companionship of at least a few good friends they can trust with their secrets and who support them and make them feel included. A good place to start is by becoming your own best friend. Decide that no one has the power to make you feel bad about yourself but you. The next step is to develop a healthy communication style.

COMMUNICATION STYLES

Your body image and self-esteem affect the way you communicate. And the type of communication you use affects your relationships with peers and potential dates. Poor communication styles include submissiveness, indirect aggression, and direct aggression. They put up barriers to strong, long-term relationships.

Submissive—or passive—communication is characterized by a sense of helplessness. It may be whiny, indecisive, and apologetic. Someone using this style routinely lets others make decisions and "goes along to get along." She always tries to please others, considers others' needs ahead of hers, and prefers not to "make waves." It's easy to see how low self-esteem encourages this type of

 ## MASLOW'S HIERARCHY OF NEEDS

Why is self-esteem important? According to a theory proposed by American psychologist Abraham Harold Maslow (1908–1970), humans share five levels of psychological needs in the following order:

1. Physiological needs for food, water, shelter, and warmth
2. Safety, stability, and freedom from fear
3. Love and belonging from friends, family, and spouse
4. Self-esteem, mastery, recognition, and respect
5. Self-actualization, from pursuing talents and creativity

According to this theory, healthy self-esteem contributes to fulfillment and helps humans become the best they can be.

communication. But, it's ineffective in letting others know your needs, wants, and opinions.

People using indirect aggression may be sarcastic, deceptive, and manipulative. They send mixed messages and try to induce guilt in others. Indirect aggression is a defense mechanism they use to protect themselves and ward off attacks from others. Again, however, it is a poor way to interact.

Finally, direct aggression comes across as bossy, arrogant, opinionated, and overbearing. It's a way to get your own way every time and gain control over another person. Bullying falls into the category of direct aggression.

MEAN GIRLS

Girls with low self-esteem are often victims of bullies. Bullying is abusive, intentional cruelty. It is a type of aggression that includes an imbalance of power, repetition, and intent to harm physically or mentally. It's a social relationship problem.

Among girls, bullying often takes the form of nasty rumors, breaking confidences, and getting others to dislike the victim. Most hurtful may be behaviors that range from simple rejection to complete exclusion from the group.

Bullying behaviors may include name-calling, teasing, or spreading rumors. These may escalate to threats, vandalism, leers and stares, and assault and battery. In high schools, bullying often takes the form of sexual harassment. Behaviors may include comments about a person's body, inappropriate touching, slurs about sexual orientation, and sexual assault.

Today's technology offers easy tools for bullies. Cyberbullying is sending embarrassing, false, or other harmful messages or images over the Internet, mobile phones, or other devices. Common examples are excessive e-mails, texts, instant messages, or postings to social network pages. Cyberbullies may ridicule another, make false comments in the person's name, or send digital pornographic material. Some cyberbullies use social media to recruit others to join in the bullying.

Bullying of all types is rampant. Some have called it a national epidemic. And no wonder. According to StompOutBullying.com, 25 percent of teens say they have been victims of bullying. And 43 percent of youths have been bullied online.

At the stage of life when others' opinions matter the most, girls who are bullied can experience loneliness, emotional distress, and severe damage to their body image and self-esteem. Some stay home from school because of it. In fact, 160,000 students stay home from school every day because of bullying, according to the National Education Association. Some beg to change schools. Some consider or commit suicide.

WHY GIRLS BULLY

Victims may be surprised to learn the reasons girls bully. One of the biggest reasons is the same desire to fit in that their victims have. Bullies gossip because they don't want to be left out of the group. They bully because others are doing it. And they bully to get "respect" from their peers. Some say

MANY GIRLS WHO BULLY WANT TO FIT IN WITH THE "IN" GROUP.
THEY GOSSIP SO THEY WON'T FEEL LEFT OUT OF THEIR GROUP
OF FRIENDS.

SE Success EATING DISORDER dieting SEXUALIZATION
TRITION body image WOMEN SELF-ESTEEM Exercise

they do it to punish people they are jealous of or because they feel better about themselves by putting others down.

Another prevalent reason girls bully is to alleviate boredom and create excitement. In short, they think it's fun. They spread rumors or embellish tales from weekend parties and enjoy the attention they get from being part of the "in group." They are desperate to belong. In reality, they

POP STAR LADY GAGA WAS A VICTIM OF BULLIES IN HIGH SCHOOL. SHE FOUNDED THE BORN THIS WAY FOUNDATION TO HELP VICTIMS, AS WELL AS BULLIES.

have serious low self-esteem issues themselves. Like their victims, they feel vulnerable and unsure of themselves.

LADY GAGA STEPS IN

Pop star Lady Gaga understands. In high school, a group of students stuffed her into a trashcan. She pretended to laugh along, but the truth is it hurt. She never told her

parents or other adults. But when a fan committed suicide, she came to realize that school age kids still suffer from bullying today. She made a commitment to help stop it.

The high-profile singer, who has sold twenty million albums and sixty-four million singles, used her celebrity capital, as well as $1.2 million in cash, to establish the Born This Way Foundation in 2012. Its purpose is to help young people who are suffering from bullying and self-confidence issues. This includes both bullies and victims. At the launch of the foundation, reported on Slate.com, she said, "There's all this focus on the victims, but the bullies are on the same playing field. They both need our help."

The foundation has teamed with the Harvard Graduate School of Education and the Berkman Center for Internet & Society to create a "new culture of kindness, bravery, acceptance, and empowerment." The MacArthur Foundation, which supports efforts to build a more peaceful world, also supports the foundation. It issued a $500,000 grant to support online and in-person programs to deter bullying and engage young people in working to stop meanness and cruelty.

ASSERTIVE COMMUNICATION

Some people think that being assertive is the same as being aggressive. However, assertive communication is the most useful way to speak—as well as listen—to others. It breaks down barriers between people.

Assertive communication expresses both positive and negative feelings in an open, direct way. People

using this style respect the rights of others. They also respect their own. They avoid judging or blaming others. And they work to solve conflicts in ways acceptable to everyone involved. The goal is to get others to treat them with respect by demonstrating that they respect themselves.

One way to do that is to use positive messages when you think and talk about yourself. In addition, avoid qualifying remarks that minimize what you're trying to say. Avoid saying such things as "That's just my idea," "If it's all right

ASSERTIVE COMMUNICATION HELPS YOU EXPRESS YOUR NEEDS AND FEELINGS, WHETHER IT IS WITH FRIENDS OR ACQUAINTANCES. IT INVOLVES STANDING UP FOR YOURSELF, AS WELL AS RESPECTING OTHERS.

USE Success EATING DISORDER dieting SEXUALIZATION
TRITION body image WOMEN SELF-ESTEEM Exercise

with you," or "Is that OK?" Don't feel the need to explain your choices. And don't apologize for your feelings or ideas. Assertive communication helps you express your needs and feelings. It eliminates the need to read another person's mind or to expect someone to read yours.

Another technique is to use "I" messages that include a statement of another's behavior, your feeling about it, and the effect on yourself when others act a certain way.

- "You make me angry" becomes "I feel angry when you …"
- "You're always late" becomes "I feel unimportant when you're late."
- "I think you…" becomes "I feel frustrated when …"
- Assertive communication eliminates the need to take responsibility for others' feelings or behaviors. Avoid "you should," "you ought to," or "you have to." Replace them with "I choose to …"

When you want something, use three steps. First say something that honors the other person's feelings. "I know you feel frustrated when…" Next, clearly state the problem and tell how you feel when it happens. Finally, clearly state what you want or what you want to see changed.

Some additional tips:

- Make eye contact.
- Stand or sit straight.
- Smile.
- Use facts, not judgments.

BULLY, THE MOVIE

The documentary *Bully*, released in 2012, draws attention to the issue of bullying through experiences of five real families in four states. Reviewers called it "wrenching," "provocative," "moving," and "troubling." *New York Times* reviewers named it a Critics' Pick.

But media buzz preceded the release. The Canadian ratings board gave it a PG rating. But the Motion Picture Association of America (MPAA) rated it R for strong language. The rating meant young moviegoers would not be admitted to theaters without parents. It also meant teachers could not show it in schools. Filmmakers cut some—but not all—profanity. They kept the "F-bombs" in an important scene where bullies harass a twelve-year-old on a school bus.

The MPAA subsequently changed its rating to PG-13.

MAKING FRIENDS

If you're shy or have trouble making friends, your communication style may be in the way. Or, you might just need a few tips.

- Smile before you speak. If you look angry or afraid, you're inhibiting conversation. Try it for a day or two. See how people react.
- Show interest in others. Ask them questions about themselves. Give them compliments you really mean.
- If someone gives you a compliment, accept it with a grateful "thank-you." Avoid the urge to put

YOU CAN BUILD FRIENDSHIPS WITH OTHERS WHO SHARE YOUR INTERESTS, LIKE THESE GIRLS WORKING ON A VASE IN A GLASS BLOWING CLASS. THERE ARE ALSO SPORTS AND CLUBS TO JOIN.

yourself down or dilute the positive attention with a negative response.

- Look for common ground. Are you an athlete? An artist? A bookworm? Look for others with the same interests. Invite them to do something with you that you'll both enjoy.
- Play a role in the conversation. Contribute your own thoughts and opinions, even if they differ from someone else's.

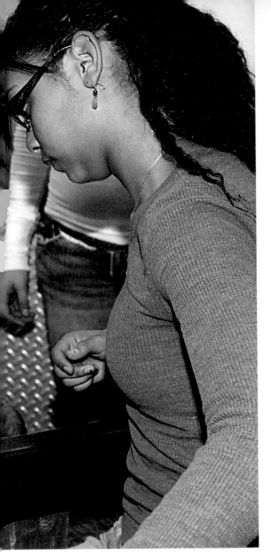

■ Be a friend. Protect secrets. Support others when they're down. Celebrate their successes.

BODY IMAGE, SELF-ESTEEM, AND DATING

One of the most troubling issues for teens with poor body image and low self-esteem revolves around dating. Girls who think they're not pretty enough or thin enough may put off potential dates with such self-conscious body language as crossed arms and slumped shoulders. Other teens base their self-worth on whether they have a mate. They are so desperate for a romantic partner to make them feel accepted, they settle for a relationship that fails to offer true respect and appreciation.

They may dress provocatively or exhibit other sexual behavior to get attention. However, as Kate Elizabeth Conner said on her blog *Lily Pads*, "If you choose to wear shirts that show off your boobs, you will attract boys. To be more specific, you will attract the kind of boys that like to look down girls' shirts."

Issues concerning body image, self-esteem, and dating are just one more way teens let others define how they value themselves. Low self-esteem is one of the main reasons for physical intimacy before being emotionally ready for it. Low self-esteem can also lead to teen promiscuity. Sex becomes a way to build confidence and feel loved, accepted, desired, and—yes—beautiful. Unfortunately, it also puts girls at risk for sexually transmitted diseases as well as mental, physical, or sexual abuse.

ABUSIVE RELATIONSHIPS

Abuse is behavior aimed at getting power and control over another person. The behavior may be mental, physical, or sexual. The abuser has little or no concern for the victim's needs. And victims often live with constant fear. They lose feelings of safety and security. Abuse that occurs in childhood and teen years often follows victims to adulthood. There, the damage from abuse affects lifelong friendships and sexual relationships.

Female abuse victims often accept some false beliefs:

- People wouldn't like me if they knew the "real" me.
- I need a man to protect me and make me whole.
- Avoiding conflict is more important than standing up for myself.
- I should not express anger.

MENTAL, PHYSICAL, AND SEXUAL ABUSE ARE AIMED AT GAINING CONTROL OVER ANOTHER. DAMAGE FROM ABUSE AFFECTS LIFELONG FRIENDSHIPS AND SEXUAL RELATIONSHIPS. BUT HELP IS AVAILABLE.

USE Success EATING DISORDER dieting SEXUALIZATION
JTRITION body image WOMEN SELF-ESTEEM Exercise

- My public image is more important than my health, safety, or self-esteem.
- Others' needs and feelings are more important than mine.

Some girls and women who believe these ideas need professional help to learn the role they play in the abuse cycle and how to change it. The good news is that they can learn how changing their behavior and view of themselves can break the cycle of abuse. They can learn that they are able to—and need to—take care of themselves and take responsibility for their own feelings. They can define themselves instead of giving that power to others. And they can revise their view of conflict and learn to stand up for themselves.

If you find yourself in an abusive situation of any kind, seek help from a school nurse, counselor, or social worker. Or, contact the abuse hotline in your state. You can also ask for help from a trusted adult or clergyperson. These resources can help refer you to professionals trained to treat victims of abuse. You can also call domestic abuse hotlines. For severe sexual abuse or rape, call the police.

MYTHS and Facts

MYTH
You're not "cool" unless you look, dress, and eat like your peers.

Fact
You're "cool" if you work toward a healthy lifestyle and accept yourself the way you are.

MYTH
Bullying has two parts: the bully and the victim.

Fact
Bullying is a dynamic problem. Some kids who are bullied go on to bully others.

MYTH
It's OK to try a new diet if the one I'm on doesn't work or if I regain weight.

Fact
Yo-yo dieting is a form of disordered eating. It can cause physical harm by slowing your metabolism. And repeated diet failures damage your self-esteem.

ABUSE EATING DISORDER
Success WOMEN
SEXUALIZATION
SELF-ESTEEM body image
dieting
NUTRITION Exercise

CHAPTER 3

SELF-INFLICTED HARM

Low self-esteem and negative body image can kill you.

That's not an exaggeration. In addition to suicides attributed to bullying and other abuse, some girls die from self-inflicted injuries that include eating disorders, self-mutilation, and cutting. Death may come from damage to the body caused by these abnormal behaviors.

An eating disorder is a life-threatening condition that involves serious physical and emotional problems along with attitudes and behaviors concerning weight and food. It is a form of addiction that is as hard to conquer as addictions to alcohol, nicotine, and other drugs. The most common eating disorders are anorexia nervosa, bulimia nervosa, and binge eating disorder (BED).

ANOREXIA NERVOSA

Anorexia nervosa is a medical diagnosis characterized by starvation. It is the most common and deadliest eating disorder. It often includes some of the following symptoms:

OBSESSIVE CONCERN WITH WEIGHT AND FOOD MAY INDICATE A LIFE-THREATENING EATING DISORDER. IF ONE OF YOUR FRIENDS SEEMS OVERLY CONCERNED WITH HER WEIGHT OR WEIGHT LOSS, SPEAK TO A TRUSTED ADULT.

USE Success EATING DISORDER dieting SEXUALIZATION
TRITION body image WOMEN SELF-ESTEEM Exercise

- Excessive influence of weight on body image or self-esteem
- Obsessive desire to be thinner
- Inability to maintain body weight at the normal range for age and height
- Significant weight loss.
- Abnormal menstrual cycle or complete cessation
- Extreme dieting

According to a study reported in 2011 in the *Archives of General Psychiatry*, lead author Jon Arcelus from the Eating Disorders Service in Leicester and Loughborough University, United Kingdom, found that among eating disorders, anorexia nervosa had the highest death rate—a full 20 percent of them from suicide. And according to Teen Health and the Media, an estimated one thousand American women die each year from anorexia nervosa alone. That number may be low. Many females with the illness actually die from such causes as cancer, cardiac arrest, failure of other organs, or other natural disorders. So they are left out of the statistics for anorexia.

For females with anorexia between the ages of fifteen and twenty-four, the mortality rate is twelve times greater than the death rate from all other causes of death in that age group, according to the National Association of Anorexia Nervosa and Associated Disorders (ANAD).

"Anorexia" literally means loss of appetite. However, anorexics are often very hungry most of the time, especially early in the process of developing the disorder. They feel better about themselves when they can overcome hunger and control what and how much they eat.

BULIMIA NERVOSA

Bulimia nervosa may occur by itself or in conjunction with anorexia nervosa. Like anorexics, teens with bulimia are trying to control their feelings. Bulimics eat huge amounts of food in a short period of time—even when they are not hungry. Then they purge.

Purging is a way to get rid of recently eaten food to keep from gaining weight. It may appear as skipped meals, excessive exercise, self-induced vomiting, or taking laxatives, enemas, or diuretics. However, it's also a way to express feelings of anger, stress, depression, or anxiety. Sometimes a dentist is the first to notice bulimic symptoms. Stomach acid from frequent vomiting erodes tooth enamel. It also damages gums, turns teeth brown, or causes sores in the mouth.

Symptoms of bulimia nervosa include:

- Use of body weight as a measure of one's value as a person
- Hiding food or eating in secret
- Frequent dieting
- Repeated episodes of binge eating followed by purging
- Lack of control while eating

Some bulimics engage in these behaviors as a way to punish themselves for unrealistic guilt. Genetic factors as

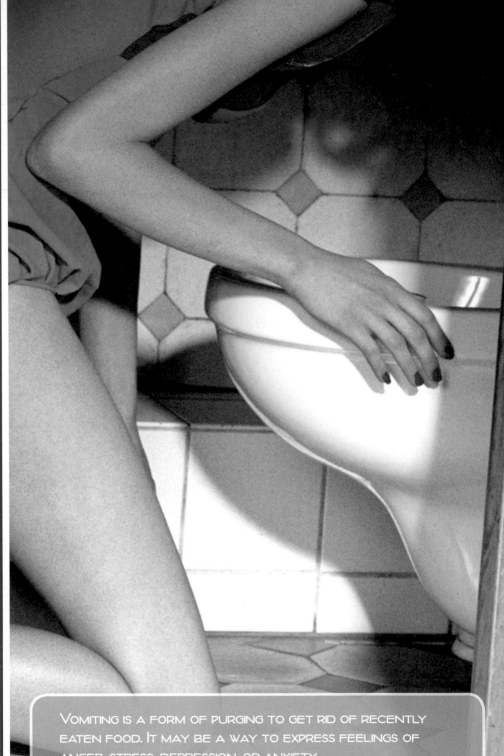

Vomiting is a form of purging to get rid of recently eaten food. It may be a way to express feelings of anger, stress, depression, or anxiety.

well as environmental ones may be involved in the development of the disorder.

BINGE EATING DISORDER

Binge eating disorder (BED) is excessive overeating. In fact, it was once known as compulsive overeating. It is often associated with obesity. According to the National Eating Disorder Information Center, about one in five obese people engage in binge eating. However, they don't compensate with purging. They may have a long history of dieting that didn't work. Genetics may predispose them to be larger or heavier than their peers.

Symptoms include:

- Frequently eating large amounts of food in a short period
- Inability to stop eating
- Eating fast or in secret
- Feeling too full after binge eating

Teens with BED often feel ashamed or embarrassed. They sometimes eat too much because they're so hungry from dieting or other food restriction. Or, they eat too much to comfort themselves. The overeating helps them ignore their feelings or avoid uncomfortable situations. BED is often associated with depression.

Although different types of eating disorders seem to have specific symptoms, the illnesses vary widely. A single individual may from time to time exhibit acts and attitudes that cross the lines among them. Another category called eating disorders not otherwise specified (EDNOS) includes combinations of signs and symptoms of all three. Defining the type of eating disorder is not as important as recognizing that a person's extreme relationship to food may have exceeded the normal range and become a mental or physical illness.

WHO GETS EATING DISORDERS?

Eating disorders have been seen in all ages and both genders from children to older adults. The distribution of the illness ranges from the age of six to seventy-six. The National Association of Anorexia Nervosa and Associated Disorders estimates that eight million or more Americans have an eating disorder, and about 90 percent of them are women. Some experts hypothesize that male cases are simply underreported since men often resist mental health help. Accurate statistics are difficult to obtain because both men and women tend to hide their problems and behaviors.

First symptoms usually appear in adolescence. While some genetic factors may be involved, events such as the death of a loved one, exposure to violence, school-related stress, and peer pressure often trigger their development. People who are perfectionists are at risk. They create such unrealistic expectations for themselves that they experience

DIET OR DISORDER?

What's the difference between a diet and an eating disorder? Some people try to lose weight so they'll be healthier. Others use food to comfort themselves or control their emotions. The reasons for the food restriction make the difference.

PEOPLE ON A DIET:
- Want to lose weight for themselves, not to please others
- Want to keep their weight under control for health reasons
- Want to lose weight in a healthy way

PEOPLE WITH EATING DISORDERS:
- Want to improve their lives by eating or not eating
- Want others' approval or negative attention
- Don't care if they damage their body by restricting their food
- Use food to deal with pain, stress, anger, and fear

frequent disappointment. Researchers have found no link between eating disorders and race or the individual's occupation, education, income, wealth, or position in society.

HIGH-PROFILE SUFFERERS

Several celebrities who have suffered from eating disorders have come forward to build awareness of the issue.

MODEL CRYSTAL RENN SUFFERED FROM ANOREXIA NERVOSA AS A TEEN. HER AGENT SUGGESTED SHE COULD MODEL FOR *VOGUE* IF SHE LOST WEIGHT. *HUNGRY* IS HER AUTOBIOGRAPHY.

CRYSTAL RENN

Former plus-size model Crystal Renn has acknowledged her battle with anorexia as a teen. Her troubles began at the age of fourteen. That's when a scout for a modeling agency told her she could model for *Vogue* fashion magazine. First, though, she had to lose 50 pounds (23 kg), a number that represented 40 percent of her body weight.

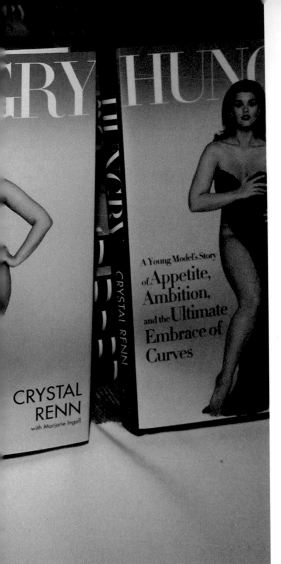

The agent also suggested that she reduce her 43-inch hips (109 cm) to 33 inches (83 cm). Renn, at first, was confident. She later told the Web site Models.com, "I thought, oh I can do that. I just have to eat healthy."

She ate healthy foods, but exercised as much as eight hours a day. She got some modeling jobs through the Ford agency, but she started regaining weight. Her agent suggested going on a diet. But she had already stopped eating sugar and fat. There was nothing "bad" left to cut. That's when she became a plus-size model.

She then changed her focus to healthy habits and maintained a healthy weight. She told MailOnline.com, "I had anorexia because ultimately, someone else set the standard for me and I wanted to follow it."

She added a comment for today's teens: "I don't want young women to think being thin is the only way to be beautiful. Beauty is not a pant size. I'm known for my body and I'm proud of my body."

Singer, dancer, and TV personality Paula Abdul serves as an ambassador for the National Eating Disorders Association. She has been treated for bulimia nervosa in the past.

ABUSE Success EATING DISORDER dieting SEXUALIZAT
NUTRITION body image WOMEN SELF-ESTEEM Exerc

Paula Abdul

Paula Abdul, a singer, choreographer, and dancer, checked herself into a clinic for treatment for bulimia nervosa in 1994. The former *American Idol* judge is an ambassador for the National Eating Disorders Association.

Her disorder started at the age of seven, but didn't develop full-blown bulimia until she was in high school. She explained that eating disorders have nothing to do with food. Instead, they're about feelings. She encourages young women with body image issues to get help.

Oprah Winfrey

Oprah Winfrey, possibly the most successful and best-known woman in the American television industry, has often spoken about her eating disorders, which include BED. She has said that food comforted her, and being heavy made her feel safe. However, she lost several jobs for being too fat. And she had several bad relationships with men that she blames on her need for approval.

In *O* magazine she said, "Getting my lifelong weight struggle under control has come from a process of treating myself as well as I treat others in every way."

SELF-INJURY

In some cases people use another approach to express emotions, relieve pain, or punish themselves for real or imagined flaws or actions. The broad disorder is known as self-injury or self-mutilation. It includes cutting, hair pulling, hitting oneself, bone breaking, and burning. The goal is to harm one's body.

The pain makes them feel better. Relief comes from the body's release of beta-endorphin. Beta-endorphin is a naturally occurring chemical produced in the brain's pituitary gland. It has better pain-killing properties than the narcotic pain reliever morphine. The body releases it in response to pain, trauma, exercise, or stress.

Cutting is the most common form of self-injury. Cutters use such tools as knives, razor blades, broken glass, or scissors to make shallow slices in the skin. Some make multiple cuts. Others make only one or two. Cutters are not trying to commit suicide. However, they can die if they accidentally cut too deeply and sever an artery. Accidents are more likely if the cutter is under the influence of alcohol or other drugs and unable to feel pain or recognize a severe injury.

Another form of self-injury is hair pulling, also known as trichotillomania. The hair puller rips hair from the scalp, eyebrows, eyelashes, or other parts of the body. Some take a lot of hair at one time. Others take only a little, but they repeat the behavior all day. Sometimes the hair does not grow back.

Self-hitting and bone breaking involve striking oneself with an object or slamming part of the body against a wall or floor. In some cases the strikes are hard enough to break one's own arm, leg, or wrist. Burning is damage to the skin with a match, candle, or other fire source. It also includes heating a metal instrument like a paper clip, fork, or knife and pressing it onto the skin.

ARTISTIC EXPRESSION

Branding, scarification, tattoos, and body piercing may also harm the body. But the goal is different. Variations of burning include branding and scarification using a hot metal applied to the skin.

Although related to burning, these activities are more closely related to artistic expression than disordered behavior. They may be done to make a "statement" or express individuality. While the practices are quite painful, the goal is to create decorative scars, not punish oneself or cause pain.

Tattooing and piercing also contain elements of pain and the risk of injury. Tattoos may become infected. Or, the recipient can have an allergic reaction to the dye or the metals used to make the jewelry for pierced holes. Use of unsterilized equipment for tattoos and piercing can spread such diseases as tetanus, tuberculosis, hepatitis, and HIV, the virus that causes AIDS.

Although the lines between them may be blurred, such body modification as tattoos, branding, or piercing for artistic reasons differs from self-injury. The biggest difference depends on whether the person makes a conscious

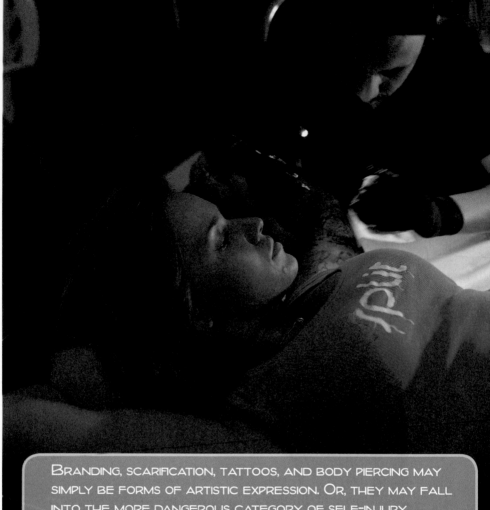

BRANDING, SCARIFICATION, TATTOOS, AND BODY PIERCING MAY SIMPLY BE FORMS OF ARTISTIC EXPRESSION. OR, THEY MAY FALL INTO THE MORE DANGEROUS CATEGORY OF SELF-INJURY DISORDERS.

decision to get the modification or if he or she cannot control the urge to do it.

Inability to deal with emotions is associated with self-injury disorders. The behaviors are ways to cope with anger, rejection, failure, loss, or helplessness. The person often feels a sense of control from the activity but strives to keep the injuries secret by hiding scars under long sleeves or long pants.

GETTING HELP

Reaching out for help is difficult, whether it's for yourself or a friend. A good place to start is with your parents, primary care doctor, religious counselor, or school nurse or social worker. You can also call hotlines for eating disorders, self-injury, and suicide.

If you suspect a friend of having one of these issues, approach him or her with kindness. Never ignore talk of suicide, even if you think your friend is joking. Tell a trusted adult right away.

In discussing possible eating or self-injury disorders, point out specific behaviors you have noticed. Explain the behaviors in terms of the symptoms of the specific illness. Emphasize that your friend may have a health problem that requires medical attention. Avoid accusing, shaming, or embarrassing your friend. And refrain from diagnosis—that's a professional's job. Instead encourage your friend to seek help.

The earlier someone gets help for an eating disorder or self-injury problem, the better the chances of reversing its

physical and emotional damage. A big roadblock, though, is the fact that people with the addictions often want to keep them. They fear losing the sense of control the disorder gives them. In a way, they feel safe with their harmful behaviors. So, even if they acknowledge a problem, they resist getting help for it.

IF YOU SUSPECT A FRIEND OF A POSSIBLE EATING OR SELF-INJURY DISORDER, POINT OUT SPECIFIC BEHAVIORS YOU HAVE NOTICED. ENCOURAGE YOUR FRIEND TO SEEK HELP.

Most people with these disorders need the help of medical or mental health professionals. These caregivers help patients discover the underlying causes of the illness and find healthy coping tools. They also guide the patient on a process of self-discovery that helps restore body image and self-esteem.

Treatment often lasts a year or more and may include psychotherapy, counseling, and self-help groups. In many cases, the entire family is involved in the process. In severe cases of life-threatening symptoms, hospitalization may be necessary. No drugs have been approved to treat eating disorders. However, some antidepressants may hold promise.

Experts advise caution in using online discussion boards for eating disorders or self-injury. The information there may be inaccurate. And advice may be harmful, including ways to hide symptoms. Posts may serve only to worsen an already bad situation.

Ten Great Questions
TO ASK A SCHOOL SOCIAL WORKER

1.
Why do self-esteem issues arise during puberty?

2.
Do boys really only like thin girls?

3.
What does treatment for an eating disorder involve?

4.
What should I do if I suspect a friend of cutting?

5.
What's wrong with teasing a classmate now and then?

6.
Why would a plastic surgeon refuse to operate on me?

7.
What's wrong with a little junk food?

8.
How can I stop others from harassing me online?

9.
How can I recognize negative or abusive people in my life?

10.
Where should I look for information about careers?

ABUSE EATING DISORDER
Success WOMEN
SEXUALIZATION
SELF-ESTEEM body image
dieting
NUTRITION Exercise

CHAPTER 4

NUTRITION AND EXERCISE

Teens often have a complex relationship with food, even if they don't have an eating disorder. The term "disordered eating" refers to a change in eating patterns that does not warrant diagnosis. The change is often due to depression or other mental illness or to a circumstance like severe homesickness.

Disordered eating may involve symptoms of anorexia, bulimia, or other diagnoses, so it's hard to tell them apart. Although disordered eating is considered less serious than full-blown eating disorders, it can still harm the body. It signals food or body image issues. A good way to tell which category the unusual eating pattern falls into is to examine motives and symptoms in terms of body image and self-esteem and the emotions that surround them.

Disordered eating might include cutting back on calories the day or two after a huge meal. Doing that to balance out calories is one thing. But if you do it because you feel guilty for having eaten too much—or for eating at all—you could be headed for trouble. Guilt, shame, or other emotional distress about what you're doing is a warning sign.

How often does the new pattern occur? If you eat too much on holidays or special occasions during the year, the behavior might be considered relatively isolated overindulgence. But if you overeat on a regular basis, you may be approaching the line between disordered eating and eating disorder. Eating behavior that causes physical harm is always suspect. However, many people with eating disorders fail to see what is happening to their bodies until the damage is severe.

Yo-yo dieting may be considered disordered eating. Yo-yo dieting is a pattern of dieting to lose weight followed by regaining the weight—or more—then dieting again. The diets restrict calories so much that the body reduces its rate of metabolism and goes into starvation mode.

Metabolism is the total of the body's chemical processes for growth, energy production, waste material elimination, and more. The slower metabolism contributes to regaining the weight once you return to a normal eating pattern. Yo-yo dieting also harms self-esteem. The person may feel like a failure for being unable to maintain a steady weight.

If you want to feel healthy, strong, and confident, a good way to start is with proper nutrition and appropriate physical activity. That's just what Queen Latifah encourages. As a celebrity client for the Jenny Craig weight management company in 2008 and 2009, Queen Latifah's message was losing weight for better health, not

As a celebrity client for the Jenny Craig weight management company, Queen Latifah promoted losing weight for better health, not to get skinny.

to get skinny. She added workouts on a treadmill and elliptical machine for an hour per day for five to seven days a week.

Achieving her weight-loss goal meant that her clothes fit better. And she had more energy. Most important to her, fans realized that her efforts were for health reasons, not an attempt to fit into a stereotyped look or size.

ABUSE Success EATING DISORDER dieting SEXUALIZA
NUTRITION body image WOMEN SELF-ESTEEM Exer

HEALTHY EATING

Moderation and variety are the keys to healthy eating habits. The purpose of a food plan is to ensure that your body gets the nutrients it needs within a daily calorie goal for weight loss, weight gain, or weight maintenance. The benefits include lower risk of heart disease, diabetes, and cancer. Try to eat different foods each week to ensure a good balance of vitamins and minerals.

So what should you eat? According to the National Heart, Lung, and Blood Institute, a healthy diet emphasizes fruits, vegetables, whole grains, and fat-free or low-fat dairy products. Protein sources include lean meat, poultry, and fish, as well as beans, eggs, and nuts. Portion size is important. A typical serving of beef, for example, should be about the size of the palm of your hand. A healthy food plan also minimizes intake of saturated fats, trans fat, cholesterol, salt, and added sugar.

A healthy diet has a good balance of carbohydrates, protein, and fat. According to Becky Hand, a licensed and registered dietitian, carbohydrates should comprise 45 percent to 65 percent of daily calories. Protein should contribute 10 percent to 35 percent. And the remaining 20 percent to 35 percent should come from fat.

TYPES OF FATS

Everyone needs some fat in the diet. Without it your body can't use the vitamins A, D, E, or K. They are fat-soluble, which means they dissolve only in fat. Fat is a source of heat and energy. It also pads and insulates nerves and organs. The four main types of fat are saturated fat, trans fat, monounsaturated fat, and polyunsaturated fat. Saturated and trans fats may be harmful. Monounsaturated and polyunsaturated fats aren't. In fact, they may actually be beneficial.

SATURATED FAT

Saturated fat comes mainly from animal food sources and causes health concerns about heart disease and diabetes. Many people think that all saturated fat comes from animal sources. Much of it does. Examples include beef, pork, poultry, whole milk, butter, cheese, and lard. However such vegetable sources as coconut oil and palm oil contain mostly saturated fat. Saturated fat is solid at room temperature.

TRANS FAT

Trans fat also comes from animal food sources. However, most of it comes from a type of food processing called

The body needs some protein, fat, and other nutrients found in meats and cheeses. However, processed products like sausage may contain trans fat that can have negative effects.

USE Success EATING DISORDER dieting SEXUALIZATION
UTRITION body image WOMEN SELF-ESTEEM Exercise

partial hydrogenation of unsaturated fats. Trans fat is also known as industrial or synthetic trans fat. It's easier to cook with and less likely to spoil than its natural counterpart. But like its saturated cousin, it poses health risks for heart disease. Trans fat is solid at room temperature.

MONOUNSATURATED FAT

Monounsaturated fat helps decrease the risk of heart disease and control insulin levels and blood sugar. Monounsaturated fat is found in olive, peanut, and canola oils. It is liquid at room temperature.

POLYUNSATURATED FAT

Polyunsaturated fat comes mostly from plant-based foods and oils, especially corn, soybean, and sunflower oils. It is also found in fish oil. Polyunsaturated fat is liquid at room temperature. It reduces the risks of heart disease and diabetes.

FATTY ACIDS

Omega-3 fatty acids are a type of polyunsaturated fat. As fat breaks down, it releases fatty acids, in the forms the body needs. Omega-3 fatty acids contribute to normal growth and development. They also help prevent obesity, bone loss, high cholesterol, high blood pressure, diabetes, cancer, depression, and other health problems.

EXPERTS RECOMMEND SEVEN SERVINGS OF FRUITS AND VEGETABLES A DAY. THE BODY MAKES MOST OF THE FATTY ACIDS IT NEEDS FROM FRUITS AND VEGETABLES.

The body makes most of the fatty acids it needs from fruits and vegetables. However, the body cannot make its own omega-3 fatty acids. These are known as the essential fatty acids. The body must get them from the food you eat. Good sources are salmon, tuna, halibut, mackerel, lake trout, herring, sardines, and other seafood. The American Heart Association recommends eating fish at least twice a week. You can also get omega-3 fatty acids from

SOME GIRLS WITH A POOR BODY IMAGE AVOID SUCH "APPEARANCE SPORTS" AS SWIMMING, FIGURE SKATING, AND GYMNASTICS BECAUSE THEY FEAR THEY'LL LOOK BAD IN THE UNIFORM.

ABUSE Success EATING DISORDER dieting SEXUALIZATI NUTRITION body image WOMEN SELF-ESTEEM Exerci

soybeans, pumpkin seeds, nut oils, soybean oil, olive oil, and garlic.

HEALTHY WEIGHT LOSS

If you are overweight for your age, height, and build, losing weight can have health benefits. The formula is easy. You need to use more calories than you take in. If you use the same number of incoming and outgoing calories, your weight will stay the same. If you eat more calories than you use, you'll gain.

According to the National Heart, Lung, and Blood Institute, to lose 1 to 2 pounds (.45 to .9 kg) per week, reduce daily intake by 500 to 1,000 calories. In general eating plans with 1,000 to 1,200 calories per day are safe for female weight loss. If you are hungry when you are on a reduced calorie diet, increase the daily number of calories by 100 to 200.

Diets using very low calorie counts of 800 calories or less should be used only with a doctor's supervision.

BODY IMAGE, SELF-ESTEEM, AND EXERCISE

A weight loss plan works best if healthy exercise accompanies it. Unfortunately, some girls with poor body image or low self-esteem avoid sports altogether. Or, they participate and risk developing eating disorders. Some girls resist physical activity. Others exercise too much. As with other aspects of body image and self-esteem, the right amount of exercise depends on the reasons for doing it.

According to the Confidence Coalition, 40 percent of girls between the ages of eleven and seventeen avoid sports because of a lack of skills. Of course, skills can be learned. You can be born with a natural talent for sports, music, or visual art. But you must develop those talents by learning the skills for those activities.

Girls with a poor body image often avoid sports because they fear they'll look bad in the uniform. This is especially true in "appearance sports," where the body is on display. Examples include swimming, figure skating, and gymnastics. Girls who participate in these types of sports have a greater risk of developing eating disorders.

For example, according to ANAD, 13 percent of girls in such sports as gymnastics and diving, where judges determine outcomes, have eating disorders. That compares with only 3 percent in sports like tennis or track that are refereed or have objective ways, like times, to determine winners. Eating disorders are also prevalent among elite female athletes. Again according to ANAD, 20 percent of top-level female athletes have eating disorders compared with 9 percent of females in general.

THE FEMALE ATHLETE TRIAD

A combination of three interrelated conditions common among female athletes is known as the female athlete triad. A girl with the triad constantly feels tired, has trouble sleeping, and often has cold hands and feet. The three types of symptoms that occur together include lack of energy, menstrual cycle disturbance, and bone loss. These symptoms vary from mild to extreme severity.

ANOREXIA ATHLETICA

Some people exercise too much. When they overexercise, they may develop a condition known as anorexia athletica, or compulsive exercise. Although it is not an official diagnosis, it has much in common with eating disorders. People with the condition try to control their bodies in an effort to gain a sense of power, control, and self-respect. Symptoms include:

- Exercising beyond the fitness level
- Taking time away from school or social activities to exercise
- Letting physical performance define value as a person
- Dissatisfaction with physical accomplishments
- Forgetting that exercise can be fun
- Overemphasizing weight and diet

Athletes need the energy from food for peak performance. In girls with the triad, low energy results from using more calories than they eat. Some athletes consciously restrict the amount of food in an effort to look thin or perform better. And sometimes this eating pattern evolves into anorexia or bulimia.

Irregular menstrual cycles can result from excessive exercise. If the athlete skips her menstrual period for three months or longer (and she's not pregnant), she has a potentially serious problem called amenorrhea.

SOME GIRLS LIKE THE CAMARADERIE OF EXERCISE CLASSES AND TEAM SPORTS. OTHERS PREFER TO WORK OUT ON THEIR OWN. EXERCISE IS AN IMPORTANT PART OF A HEALTHY LIFESTYLE.

Athletes who have the triad risk losing bone mass. This can lead to weakened bones. The athlete may suffer stress fractures or broken bones. Over time she may develop osteoporosis, a condition where bones become brittle from loss of protein and minerals—notably calcium.

RISK FACTORS FOR THE TRIAD

Being a gymnast, figure skater, ballet dancer, distance

runner, swimmer, or diver may place too much emphasis on a lean figure. Such athletes are at risk for developing the triad. Other risk factors include:

- Participating in such sports as boxing that require weight checks
- Attending so many sporting events that they interfere with social life
- Exercising beyond normal workouts for the sport
- Feeling pressure to win no matter what
- Feeling—or being— punished for gaining weight
- Dealing with controlling coaches or parents

HEALTHY EXERCISE

A healthy exercise program focuses on health, not weight loss. It's part of a rewarding lifestyle.

You can choose from a wide variety of activities, from organized sports to working out alone. Some

WHEN CHOOSING AN ATHLETIC ACTIVITY, LOOK FOR ONE THAT'S FUN SO YOU'LL STAY AT IT. IF IT FEELS LIKE A CHORE, YOU'LL LIKELY START AVOIDING THE EXERCISE YOU NEED.

girls like the shared companionship of team sports. Others prefer individual sports like swimming or tennis or noncompetitive activities like biking or snowboarding.

In choosing an activity, keep in mind that the best exercise is the one you'll do. If it feels like a chore, you'll likely drop out. If it's fun, you'll stay at it.

USE Success EATING DISORDER dieting SEXUALIZATION
JTRITION body image WOMEN SELF-ESTEEM Exercise

THE THREE ELEMENTS OF FITNESS

A healthy body has three elements: endurance, strength, and flexibility. All three are important to your fitness. You build endurance with aerobic exercise. Aerobic exercise is any activity that quickens your breathing and heart rate. It is called aerobic because it involves the systems that deliver oxygen to the body. Activities that build endurance include swimming, running, biking, hiking, and fast walking.

Strength training also contributes to endurance. The stronger your muscles, the longer you can exercise without getting worn out. Strength training also helps athletes in many sports develop enough strength to perform required skills. Strong muscles also prevent injury by supporting the joints involved in athletic movement. Examples of strength training include such weight-bearing exercises as pull-ups, push-ups, crunches, squats, and leg raises. Sports that develop strength include rowing, cross-country skiing, biking, and skating.

Flexibility means that you can stretch or bend with ease. It protects the body from muscle strains and sprains and improves athletic performance. Stretching exercises encourage flexibility. Activities that increase flexibility include martial arts, ballet, gymnastics, and yoga. After any type of exercise, it's good to perform stretching exercises specific to the arms, legs, back, and neck.

EXERCISE BENEFITS

With good health as the motivating factor, exercise increases the physical and mental aspects of your life.

Here are some of the ways you benefit from physical activity:

- Exercise feels good. That's because it releases the same pain-killing endorphins some people seek from negative activities like cutting and hair pulling.
- Exercise improves attitude. The feeling of accomplishment from achieving sports or fitness goals helps raise self-esteem.
- Fitness improves physical appearance. It helps you reach and maintain a healthy weight.
- Exercise improves overall health. It reduces risk factors for such diseases as high blood pressure, type 2 diabetes, and heart disease.

ABUSE   EATING DISORDER

Success   WOMEN

SEXUALIZATION

SELF-ESTEEM   body image

dieting

NUTRITION   Exercise

CHAPTER 5

SUCCESS IN LIFE

Lifelong success depends on positive self-esteem and body image. If yours are negative, try to change your thinking. Guess what? The best person to help you is you! You may need help from friends, parents, or professionals to empower yourself. But you can do a lot on your own.

Try to step back and see yourself objectively. You can go a long way toward improving self-esteem by using positive self-talk instead of criticizing yourself. Refrain from such self-talk as "I don't matter," "Nobody likes me," or "I'm not good enough." Instead, make a conscious choice to send encouraging messages: I can do this. I'm a good person. If I make mistakes, I'll try again. Whenever bad thoughts creep in, replace them with something positive.

Make three lists: what you like to do, what you're good at, and what you'd like to do (now or in the future). Add to the lists as you think of more items. Focus on the things you're good at. You might be surprised how many things you do well.

Low self-esteem often comes from fear of failure. What better way to overcome that fear than to prove yourself wrong? Focus on what you're good at instead of dwelling on your past mistakes. Set realistic, specific goals and work toward them. When you succeed, celebrate the achievement. Look at setbacks realistically. They usually aren't the end of the world. Learn from failure. What could you have done better? If you think of something, change it. If you did your best, well, that's victory in itself.

You can also build self-esteem by trying something new. Take a chance, and expect a good outcome. Force yourself to be more outgoing. Stop comparing yourself to others. You are "good enough" just the way you are. And stop feeling jealous—yes, you can control that— of what other kids have. Remember that who you are is more important than what you have. Be grateful for who you are.

CREATIVITY BUILDS CONFIDENCE

Everyone is creative in one way or another. Perhaps you haven't discovered your hidden talents. If you're interested in something, it's a sign that you may have a talent for it. Be bold. Explore it. That doesn't mean you must rush out and compose a symphony or write a novel. You can start small and dabble in several activities.

Sign up for lessons or workshops. Forgive yourself if you aren't an expert at first. You'll likely have to practice to get better. You don't have to limit yourself to typical "artsy-craftsy" activities like art, music, photography, or writing. You may have a talent for the hula hoop, working with

children, tending a garden, or organizing.

The more things you try, the better chance you'll find a creative outlet. Remember, you don't have to be perfect to express your creative self. Avoid judging your output. Let yourself have fun doing it.

Just Do It

You can build self-esteem simply by doing things. Lots of them. A wide variety of activities adds to your life experience. Try new things, even in such areas traditionally dominated by boys as construction, science, or computer projects.

Participate in school activities. Go to the bonfire. Support school teams by attending games. Join the yearbook staff, chess club, or fashion club. If there's no club for your interests, start one. Attend the youth group at your place of worship. Join the choir.

Invent your own field trips to places of interest in your area—and beyond. Interested in space travel? Plan a trip to space camp. Do you love animals? Help out at pet adoption events. Want to share your musical ability? Hold a summer music camp for the kids in your neighborhood.

LOOK FOR A CREATIVE OUTLET. YOU MAY HAVE A TALENT FOR GARDENING, MUSIC, OR VISUAL ART. TRY NEW THINGS. YOU DON'T HAVE TO BE PERFECT TO HAVE FUN.

Ask a parent or teacher to help you arrange to meet professionals in a field you're interested in. You can also volunteer for community work. If you're interested in medicine, volunteer at a hospital. If you love books, see if you can help at the library. Your community has many areas you could help out in. See what you'd like to do. Look into organizations like Big Brothers and Big Sisters. Coach a youth sports team.

GRAMMY AWARD–WINNING SINGER ADELE ADMITS TO HAVING INSECURITIES IN HER LIFE. BUT SHE SAYS SHE WON'T HANG OUT WITH PEOPLE WHO POINT THEM OUT.

IGNORE NEGATIVITY

Some other ways to build self-esteem are within your control. Avoid negative situations. Who needs them? Hang out with positive people whenever you can. Practice saying positive things to others and yourself. If your "friends" always seem to bring you down, change your friends.

Grammy Award–winning singer Adele understands: "I've seen people where (appearance) rules their lives, who want to be thinner or have bigger boobs, and how it wears them down," she told *Rolling Stone*. "And I don't want that in my life. I have insecurities, of course, but I don't hang out with anyone who points them out to me."

Instead, pay attention to the good things in your life. Keep a journal. Write down only positive happenings.

As you participate in new activities, you'll have fun. You'll also find others who share your interests. Some of them may become new friends. You may even develop the sense of belonging that all people need.

REPAIRING BODY IMAGE

You can also take control of your body image. As with self-esteem, the first step is to stop thinking negative thoughts. If they creep in, switch to a part of your body that you like. Or, think about something else entirely.

For Sara Ramirez of *Grey's Anatomy*, the process is ongoing. "I still have days when I walk by the mirror on my way to the shower and think, 'oh God, I didn't just see that!'" she told *Glamour*. "But I've learned to stop myself and ask, am I being realistic?"

TO IMPROVE YOUR SELF-ESTEEM, FOCUS ON YOUR TALENTS AND ABILITIES, LIKE BASKETBALL OR OTHER SPORTS, INSTEAD OF YOUR APPEARANCE. REFRAIN FROM TELLING YOURSELF NEGATIVE MESSAGES.

Instead of focusing on your looks, think about the movement that your body lets you do. Are you good at free throws or hip-hop dancing? Do you like bowling or walks in the park? Be grateful for your physical abilities.

Ramirez asks herself, "What do I love about my body? What am I grateful for? The answers to those questions remind me that I'm very blessed."

Recognize that your value as a person has nothing to do with your appearance. Stop comparing your body

to others'—especially unrealistic television, film, and magazine images you see. Don't compare your body to your peers' either. As a teen, your body is still developing. Different people have a different genetic makeup, as well as different lifestyles and other environmental factors. Their body changes are likely coming at different times from yours. Consider yourself a work in progress.

Be realistic about what you can change and what you can't. Take steps to change what you can in healthy ways. You can't change your height, eye color, or shoe size. Accept those things. Remember, there is no ideal body type, size, or shape. Instead, accept the diversity. Include yourself. Instead of emphasizing appearance, take responsibility for taking care of your body. Work toward good health.

As you explore ways to build self-esteem and a positive body image, you don't have to go it alone. Life can

USE Success EATING DISORDER dieting SEXUALIZATION
UTRITION body image WOMEN SELF-ESTEEM Exercise

GIRLS TAKING CHARGE

Males seem to dominate the world of longboarding. But girls like to skate, too. And they don't like their minority status among mostly male crews. That's why a group of girls founded the Longboard Girls Crew (LGC). It's an international online community of girls who like to skate together. Their Web site has become a place where girls in the sport can meet, share tips, arrange meetings, or start their own local crews. It also has regular updates about upcoming events and competitions that girls can participate in.

Even though girls have used skateboards since the 1960s, many people are still surprised to see them skate. One of LGC's goals is to raise public awareness about past, present, and future girls' roles in longboarding. But LGC is not a girls-only site. Guys are welcome, too.

sometimes seem overwhelming. If you feel that way, ask for help. If that doesn't work—or if your problems are serious—you may need to talk to a professional. Don't hesitate to seek help if you need it.

LOOK FOR POSITIVE ROLE MODELS

If you've been misled by media images, look for positive role models outside the stereotypes. Katie Davidson is one. As a high school sophomore she was a placekicker on the eight-"man" football team at Community Christian School near Atlanta, Georgia.

She was nominated for homecoming queen, but that posed a problem. School rules required girls who were potential members of the homecoming court to wear a dress to the game. Her football uniform didn't qualify. School officials amended the rules to read that the girls had to wear "a dress or football uniform." She was named a homecoming princess.

Sejal Hathi is another teen role model. At age fifteen she founded the international nonprofit organization Girls Helping Girls (GHG) in Fremont, California. The group has helped thousands of girls in more than twenty countries improve their communities, start small businesses, and address global issues.

The group has raised money to provide computers, school supplies, and scholarships or funding for girls and women to use for education or starting their own businesses. GHG also funded a new library in India. In an interview with the *Contra Costa Times*, she said, "Whenever I think of something, I think big."

Hathi coauthored her first book about entrepreneurship at the age of sixteen. She has been recognized by media outlets, organizations, and corporations, as well as the U.S. secretary of education and the president of the United States for her academic as well as extracurricular achievements.

But she doesn't call herself a hero. In the *Contra Costa Times* interview, she said, "My heroes are the millions of girls in developing countries who walk those 10 miles to school every day, who have to take care of their siblings every day, who can't go to school, who work on their family farm, who have to get married before age 18 yet still keep on striving, still keep on dreaming, still keep on seeking a better life. Those are my heroes because they teach me that anything is possible and that all human beings are valuable."

GIRLS WIN SCIENCE FAIR

No one talked about beauty or physical appearance when three teenage girls won the grand prizes in their age groups in the international 2011 Google Science Fair. The results made news because girls in the United States traditionally shy away from careers in science.

PRESIDENT BARACK OBAMA CONGRATULATES SEVENTEEN-YEAR-OLD SHREE BOSE, OF FORT WORTH, TEXAS, FOR WINNING THE 2011 GOOGLE SCIENCE FAIR. AMERICAN GIRLS ARE OFTEN UNDERREPRESENTED IN CAREERS IN MATH AND SCIENCE.

ABUSE Success EATING DISORDER dieting SEXUALIZAT
NUTRITION body image WOMEN SELF-ESTEEM Exerc

According to a study reported in 2010 by researchers from Florida Gulf Coast University and the University of Colorado at Boulder, men outnumbered women 73 percent to 27 percent in all sectors of employment for science and engineering. The study, *Women in Science, Technology, Engineering, and Math*, also found that "many girls who take advanced science courses in middle school do not continue to study science in high school."

So observers were surprised when all three top prizes went to American girls. They excelled in a field often dominated by their male counterparts. Seventeen-year-old Texan Shree Bose won in the seventeen-to-eighteen-year-old category for her research on a chemotherapy drug commonly used to treat ovarian cancer. She discovered a protein that may prevent the development of resistance to the drug over time.

Naomi Shah from Oregon won in the fifteen-to-sixteen-year-old age group. She studied the effects of air quality on people who have asthma. In the thirteen-to-fourteen-year-old age group, Lauren Hodge from Pennsylvania won for studying the effects marinades used for grilling meat have on the levels of cancer-causing chemicals produced in the cooking process.

♀ CHANGE YOUR WORLD

Dream big. Would you like to travel abroad and learn about other cultures? You can have fun and meet local citizens in such places as South Africa, China, Costa Rica, and Italy as a People to People student ambassador.

For nearly fifty years, People to People has "bridge[d] cultural and political borders through education and exchange, making the world a better place for future generations."

Student ambassadors represent their school, community, state, and country to other people around the world. For more information, visit their Web site (http://www .peopletopeople.com).

You may not share any of these teen role models' interests, but you can see them as examples of what girls like you can do. It's possible to make your dreams come true.

YOU'RE ENTITLED TO DREAM

American poet Carl Sandburg once said, "Nothing happens unless first we dream." Do you have dreams? Goals you'd like to pursue? Try this: If you had the money, talent, skills, and opportunity to do anything you wanted, what would that be? Go ahead, be outrageous. Make a list.

You might be surprised to learn that simply by writing down your dreams, you are taking the first step toward making them come to pass. Accomplishing your goals won't be easy. You'll face obstacles that may seem impossible to overcome. But stay persistent. Work hard. And keep your dreams alive.

A Compass to Guide You

The leadership compass developed by PEARLS for Teen Girls Inc., can show you the way. The nonprofit leadership development organization in Milwaukee, Wisconsin, helps girls ages ten to nineteen "use their personal power to achieve their dreams and goals."

The five-point compass leads to the self-development of "heart, mind, body, and spirit" that is essential to happiness and well-being. The five points, known as the PEARLS Promise include:

1. **Loving myself:** Adopt an I-can-do-it attitude. Take care of myself. Try new things. Build confidence. Discover myself.
2. **Building relationships:** Appreciate others who are different from me. Trust reasons behind what others do. Be understanding of others. Communicate with respect and kindness.
3. **Striving to achieve:** Improve my grades. Read for fun. Do my best. Be motivated to learn—now and throughout my life.
4. **Believing that the sky's the limit:** Dream big. Be open to possibilities about my future. Find information about careers. Explore ways to make my dreams come true.

5. **Helping hands in the community:** Volunteer my time and talents. Get involved in a problem-solving project. Show interest in needs beyond my own neighborhood.

DREAM BIG. THEN TAKE STEPS TO MAKE YOUR DREAMS COME TRUE. IT WON'T BE EASY, BUT IF YOU STAY PERSISTENT AND WORK HARD, YOU'LL BE SURPRISED AT WHAT YOU ACCOMPLISH.

Even though the organization primarily focuses on African American and Latina girls, the guide serves all girls everywhere. Especially you.

USE Success EATING DISORDER dieting SEXUALIZATION
UTRITION body image WOMEN SELF-ESTEEM Exercise

abuse Behavior aimed at getting power and control over another person.

anorexia nervosa An eating disorder characterized by an intense fear of gaining weight or being fat, leading to malnutrition and severe weight loss.

assertive communication Social interaction where the parties express both positive and negative feelings in an open, direct way.

beta-endorphin A natural body chemical produced in the brain in response to pain, trauma, exercise, or stress.

binge eating Out-of-control consumption of huge amounts of food.

body image The way one feels about her physical appearance.

bulimia Eating disorder characterized by binge eating followed by purging.

bullying A type of verbal or physical aggression that includes an imbalance of power, intent to harm, and repetition.

cyberbullying Sending embarrassing, false, or harmful messages or images over the Internet, mobile phones, or other devices.

diuretic A drug or other substance that reduces the amount of water in the body by increasing the amount of urination.

eating disorders not otherwise specified (EDNOS) Medical conditions that include combinations of signs and symptoms of anorexia, bulimia, or binge eating.

indirect aggression A communication style that is sarcastic, deceptive, or manipulative.

morphine A potentially addictive narcotic pain medication made from opium.

obesity A weight more than 20 percent higher than an individual's ideal body weight for height, age, gender, and build because of abnormal accumulation of body fat.

objectification Thinking of or presenting something as an object.

purging To force consumed food or calories out of the body to keep from gaining weight.

self-esteem The way one values herself.

self-injury A way to express or relieve pain or punish oneself. It may include cutting, burning, branding, or hitting oneself with an object or against a wall or floor.

sexualization An emphasis on sexual appeal or behavior in determining self-worth without regard for any other characteristics.

submissive communication Social interaction characterized by a sense of passive helplessness. It may come across as whiny, indecisive, and apologetic.

trichotillomania Hair pulling as a form of self-injury.

American Academy of Nutrition and Dietetics
216 West Jackson Boulevard, Suite 800
Chicago, IL 60606
(800) 366-1655
Web site: http://www.eatright.org
The American Academy of Nutrition and Dietetics is a
    national organization of food and nutrition profession-
    als. Formerly known as the American Dietetic
    Association.

BullyingCanada
471 Smythe Street
P.O. Box 27009
Fredericton, NB E3B 9M1
Canada
(877) 352-4497
Web site: http://www.bullyingcanada.ca
BullyingCanada is a registered charity that connects youth
    who speak out about bullying and victimization and who
    want to help stop bullying.

Diamond In The Rough (DITR)
2140 McGee Road, Suite C-640
Snellville, GA 30078
(678) 376-9676
Web site: http://www.ditr.org

DITR is a faith-based, nondenominational organization that builds self-esteem, character, and leadership through preventive programs and enrichment activities.

Girls Action Foundation
24 Mont Royal West, Suite 601
Montreal, QC H2T 2S2
Canada
(888) 948-1112
Web site: http://girlsactionfoundation.ca
Girls Action Foundation is a Canadian nonprofit organization that supports more than three hundred organizations and reaches more than sixty thousand girls and young women through programs that offer empowerment, leadership, and community action opportunities.

Girls Circle Association
458 Christensen Lane
Cotati, CA 94931
(707) 794-9477
Web site: http://www.girlscircle.com
Girls Circle Association is a project of the Tides Center. It seeks to encourage the development of strength, courage, confidence, honesty, and communication skills for girls. Its goal is to help girls take full advantage of their

talents, academic interests, career pursuits, and potential for healthy relationships.

Girls Helping Girls
P.O. Box 200653
New Haven, CT 06520
(510) 592-4466
Web site: http://www.empoweragirl.org
Girls Helping Girls is an international nonprofit organization based in the San Francisco Bay area. It matches American girls with girls in developing countries, who work together to identify community problems.

National Association of Anorexia Nervosa and Associate Disorders (ANAD)
800 E. Diehl Road, #160
Naperville, IL 60563
(847) 831-3438
Web site: http://www.anad.org
ANAD is a national nonprofit organization that works to prevent and ease such eating disorders as anorexia nervosa, bulimia nervosa, and binge eating disorder.

Weight Watchers International, Inc.
300 Jericho Quadrangle, Suite 350
Jericho, NY 11753

(800) 651-6000
Web site: http://www.weightwatchersinternational.com
Weight Watchers is an international provider of weight
   management and healthy lifestyle development
   services.

WEB SITES

Due to the changing nature of Internet links, Rosen
Publishing has developed an online list of Web sites
related to the subject of this book. This site is updated
regularly. Please use this link to access the list:

http://www.rosenlinks.com/WOM/Body

Beck, Debra. *My Feet Aren't Ugly: A Girl's Guide to Loving Herself from the Inside Out*. New York, NY: Beaufort Books, 2011.

Brande, Robin. *Fat Cat*. New York, NY: Knopf, 2009.

Brotherton, Marcus, and Mary Margaret Brotherton. *Blur: A Graphic Reality Check for Teens Dealing with Self-Image*. New York, NY: Multnomah Books, 2010.

Capacchione, Lucia. *The Creative Journal for Teens: Making Friends with Yourself*. Franklin Lakes, NJ: The Career Press Inc., 2008.

Chow, Cara. *Bitter Melon*. New York, NY: Scholastic, 2011.

Crane, E. M. *Skin Deep*. New York, NY: Delacorte Books for Young Readers, 2008.

Gay, Kathlyn. *Body Image and Appearance: The Ultimate Teen Guide* (It Happened to Me). Lanham, MD: Scarecrow Press, 2009.

Headley, Justina Chen. *North of Beautiful*. New York, NY: Little, Brown Books for Young Readers, 2010.

Hogan, Mary. *Pretty Face*. New York, NY: HarperTeen, 2008.

McLinden, Shannon. *The Me Nobody Knew*. Minneapolis, MN: Carolrhoda Books, 2010.

Mysko, Claire. *Girls Inc. Presents: You're Amazing!: A No-Pressure Guide to Being Your Best Self*. Avon, MA: Adams Media, 2008.

Rooney, Anne. *Bullying*. London, England: Arcturus Publishing, 2010.

Rosenwald, Laurie. *All the Wrong People Have Self-Esteem: An Inappropriate Book for Young Ladies*. New York, NY: Bloomsbury USA, 2008.

Ryan, Peter. *Online Bullying* (Teen Mental Health). New York, NY: Rosen Publishing, 2011.

Salter, Sydney. *My Big Nose and Other Natural Disasters*. New York NY: Graphia, 2009.

Shallit, Wendy. *The Good Girl Revolution: Young Rebels with Self-Esteem and High Standards*. New York, NY: Ballantine Books, 2008.

Silverman, Robyn, and Dina Santorelli. *Good Girls Don't Get Fat: How Weight Obsession Is Messing Up Our Girls and How We Can Help Them Thrive Despite It*. Toronto, ON, Canada: Harlequin, 2010.

Silver-Stock, Carrie. *Secrets Girls Keep: What Girls Hide (& Why) and How to Break the Stress of Silence*. Deerfield Beach, FL: HCI Teens, 2010.

Siobhan, Vivian. *Same Difference*. New York, NY: Scholastic, 2010.

Swigget, Chelsea. *Rae: My True Story of Fear, Anxiety, and Social Phobia* (Louder Than Words). Deerfield Beach, FL: HCI Teens, 2010.

Barker, Joanne. "Food and Your Body." WebMD.com, 2010. Retrieved March 3, 2012 (http://teens.webmd .com/girls-puberty-10/girls-eatingdisorders?print=true).

Center on Media and Child Health. "How Do Magazines Affect Body Image?" Education.com, 2011. Retrieved March 3, 2012 (http://www.education.com/print /how-magazines-affect-body-image).

Dove.Us. "The Dove Campaign for Real Beauty." Retrieved March 31, 2012 (http://www.dove.us/Social -Mission/campaign-for-real-beauty.aspx).

Engel, Beverly. *The Nice Girl Syndrome*. Hoboken, NJ: John Wiley & Sons, 2008.

Erenza, Jen. "Miley Cyrus & Demi Lovato Fight Fat Talk Together." RyanSecrest.com, December 1, 2011. Retrieved March 31, 2012 (http://ryanseacrest.com /2011/12/01/miley-cyrus-demi-lovato-fight-fat -talk-together).

Feigenbaum, Naomi. *Maintaining Recovery from Eating Disorders*. Philadelphia, PA: Jessica Kingsley Publishers, 2012.

Female-Puberty.com. "Low Self-Esteem Signs." Retrieved March 3, 2012 (http://www.female-puberty.com /LowSelfEsteemSigns.html).

Fleming, Olivia. "Was Jennifer Lawrence Too FAT for the *Hunger Games*? Critics Believe Actress Should Have Looked 'More Hungry.'" Mail Online, March 28, 2012. Retrieved March 30, 2012 (http://www.dailymail

.co.uk/femail/article-2121740/Was-Jennifer-Lawrence
-FAT-Hunger-Games-Male-critics-believe-actress-looked
-hungry.html?ito=feeds-newsxml).

Gurion, Anita. "How to Raise Girls with Healthy Self-
Esteem." NYU Child Study Center. Retrieved March 3,
2012 (http://www.education.com/reference/article
/Ref_Mirror_Mirror_Wall).

Kiley, David. "*Mad Men* Star Christina Hendricks the New
Face of Vivienne Westwood." Luxist.com, March 2,
2011. Retrieved April 1, 2012 (http://www.luxist
.com/2011/03/02/mad-men-star-christina-hendricks
-the-new-face-of-vivienne-westwo).

Lukash, Frederick N. *The Safe and Sane Guide to Teenage
Plastic Surgery*. Dallas, TX: BenBella Books, 2010.

MayoClinic.com. "Healthy Body Image: Tips for Guiding Girls."
June 5, 2010. Retrieved March 4, 2012 (http://www
.mayoclinic.com/health/healthy-body-image/MY01225).

National Association of Anorexia Nervosa and Associated
Disorders. "Eating Disorders Statistics." Retrieved March
31, 2012 (http://www.anad.org/get-information
/about-eating-disorders/eating-disorders-statistics).

Paul, Pamela. "The Playground Gets Even Tougher." *New
York Times*, October 8, 2010. Retrieved November
16, 2011 (http://www.nytimes.com/2010/10/10
/fashion/10Cultural.html?pagewanted=all).

Raiten-D'Antonio, Toni. *Ugly as Sin*. Deerfield Beach, FL:
Health Communications, 2010.

Silverthorne, Elizabeth. *Anorexia and Bulimia*. Farmington Hills, MI: Lucent Books, 2010.

Swearer, Susan M., Dorothy L. Espelage, and Scott Napolitano. *Bullying Prevention and Intervention: Realistic Strategies for Schools*. New York, NY: The Guilford Press, 2009.

Tapper, Christina. "Queen Latifah Achieves Weight-Loss Goal." People.com, June 17, 2008. Retrieved April 2, 2012 (http://www.people.com/people/article /0,,20207156,00.html).

Teen Health and the Media. "Body Image and Nutrition." Retrieved March 3, 2012 (http://www.depts.washington .edu/thmedia/view.cgi?section=bodyimage&page +fastfacts).

TeensHealth.org. "Body Image and Self-Esteem." May 2009. Retrieved Nov. 16, 2011 (http://kidshealth .org/teen/your_mind/body_image/body_image.html).

Wiseman, Rosalind. *Queen Bees and Wannabees: Helping Your Daughter Survive Cliques, Gossip, Boyfriends, and the New Realities of Girl World*. New York, NY: Three Rivers Press, 2009.

Withers, Jennie, and Phyllis Hendrickson. *Hey, Back Off!: Tips for Stopping Teen Harassment*. Far Hills, NJ: New Horizon Press, 2011.

ABOUT THE AUTHOR

Mary-Lane Kamberg is an award-winning professional writer specializing in nonfiction for juveniles and adults. She has published twenty-two books, including thirteen for young readers. She is co-leader of the Kansas City Writers Group and belongs to the Midwest Children's Authors Guild. She coaches club swimming for the Kansas City Blazers.

PHOTO CREDITS

Cover, back cover, pp. 10, 26, 44, 64, 82 © iStockphoto.com/ Maridav; pp. 6–7 © iStockphoto.com/Summer Derrick; p. 11 Eric Charbonneau/WireImage/Getty Images; pp. 12-13 Jim Spellman/ WireImage/Getty Images; pp. 14–15 Juice Images/Cultura/Getty Images; pp. 20-21 Dove/Press Association via AP Images; p. 23 Erik C. Pendzich/Rex USA, courtesy Everett Collection; p. 27 Britt Erlanson/The Image Bank/Getty Images; p. 31 Digital Vision/ Photodisc/Getty Images; pp. 32–33, 72–73 Boston Globe/Getty Images; pp. 34–35 Jupiterimages/Brand X Pictures/Getty Images; pp. 38–39, 66–67, 84–85 © AP Images; p. 41 © iStockphoto. com/Alexey Tkachenko; p. 45 Wavebreak Media/Thinkstock; pp. 48–49 Kalle Singer/Getty Images; pp. 52–53 Duffy-Marie Arnoult/ WireImage/Getty Images; pp. 54–55 Jeffrey Mayer/WireImage/ Getty Images; pp. 58–59 © Sun-Sentinel/ZUMA Press; pp. 60–61 Ingram Publishing/Thinkstock; pp. 69, 76–77 iStockphoto/ Thinkstock; pp. 70–71 © iStockphoto .com/Baloncici; pp.78–79 © iStockphoto.com/technotr; p. 86 Jeff Kravitz/FilmMagic/Getty Images; pp. 88–89 The Washington Post/ Getty Images; pp. 92–93 McClatchy-Tribune/Getty Images; pp. 96–97 Brand X Pictures/Thinkstock.

Designer: Nicole Russo; Editor: Bethany Bryan; Photo Researcher: Amy Feinberg